© **POSITIVE WORDS FOR YOU**
BY SANDEEP RAVIDUTT SHARMA

Table of Contents

Introduction IV

Positive Words For You..1

© POSITIVE WORDS FOR YOU
BY SANDEEP RAVIDUTT SHARMA

Introduction

This book provides you with a list of **100 motivational quotes and thoughts** focussing mainly on improving your wellness quotient. Ask yourself whether you are happy? If not, you should pursue those aspects of your life which can make you happy. Remember happiness is a state of mind, in the same situation at different points of time you can be unhappy or happy. The usage of positive words when you think, speak or write, can very well influence your actions on the ground. Embrace positive thoughts and be happy. I'm sure if you keep reading, referring, sharing these thoughts and quotes, you may derive inspiration and develop a good understanding of various business perspectives and facts.

"The positive words have got the power to heal and inspire."

I sincerely hope, you will find this book amazing, interesting, rejuvenating, unique and a constant source of inspiration.

Thank You and Happy Reading.

© POSITIVE WORDS FOR YOU
BY SANDEEP RAVIDUTT SHARMA

© Copyright 2018 Sandeep Ravidutt Sharma - All rights reserved.
In no way is it legal to reproduce, duplicate, or transmit any part of this document in either electronic means or in printed format. Recording of this publication is strictly prohibited and any storage of this document is not allowed unless with written permission from the publisher. All rights reserved. The information provided herein is stated to be truthful and consistent, in that any liability, in terms of inattention or otherwise, by any usage or abuse of any policies, processes, or directions contained within is the solitary and utter responsibility of the recipient reader. Under no circumstances will any legal responsibility or blame be held against the author / publisher for any reparation, damages, or monetary loss due to the information herein, either directly or indirectly. The author own all copyrights.
Legal Notice:
This book is copyright protected. This is only for personal use. You cannot amend, distribute, sell, use, quote or paraphrase any part or the content within this book without the consent of the author or copyright owner. Legal action will be pursued if this is breached.
Disclaimer Notice:
Please note the information contained within this book is for motivational, educational and knowledge sharing purpose only. Every attempt has been made to provide the reader accurate, up to date and reliable complete information. No warranties of any kind are expressed or implied. Readers acknowledge that the author is not engaging in the rendering of legal, financial, medical or professional advice. By reading this document, the reader agrees that under no circumstances the author / publisher is responsible for any losses, direct or indirect, which are incurred as a result of the use of information contained within this document, including, but not limited to, —errors, omissions, or inaccuracies.

If you have further questions, contact on
Tel: +919969256731
Email: sandeepraviduttsharma@gmail.com

© **POSITIVE WORDS FOR YOU**
BY SANDEEP RAVIDUTT SHARMA

Dedication

This book is dedicated to **Goddess Bhairavi**. In the Hindu religion, the Goddess Bhairavi represents divine anger and wrath which is directed towards impurities within us as well as to the negative forces that obstructs our spiritual growth. Bhairavi Mata is also called as **Shubhamkari** and does good things. She is often depicted in images as holding a book, rosary and making abhaya and varada mudra with her hands. She is fiercely protective, lending us wisdom and power, steadiness and clarity. She personifies light and fire, supporting us to reveal what we keep hidden and inviting us to explore our hidden mind and any secret darkness.
 I hereby recite the following Bhairavi mool mantra...
"Om Hreem Bhairavi Kalaum Hreem Svaha"
And pray to **Goddess Bhairavi** for lending wisdom and power, steadiness and clarity in the life of my readers and the world. May Goddess Bhairavi protect us from negative forces along with removing impurities of our mind.

POSITIVE WORDS FOR YOU

© **POSITIVE WORDS FOR YOU**
BY SANDEEP RAVIDUTT SHARMA

Choosing the straight path doesn't guarantee you reaching the destination but makes you feel proud about having followed the righteous path.

You don't need anyone else to predict your future. Your hands and mind are good and powerful enough to make your future.

Thoughts on their own have nothing to do with being positive or negative. It's how we respond to a given situation makes it positive or negative. Respond constructively.

© POSITIVE WORDS FOR YOU
BY SANDEEP RAVIDUTT SHARMA

Success awaits those who have taken the right step forward.

© **POSITIVE WORDS FOR YOU**
BY SANDEEP RAVIDUTT SHARMA

Your win announces the world that you have arrived. And with your shining and glorious efforts you can further assure them that you are going to stay.

© **POSITIVE WORDS FOR YOU**
BY SANDEEP RAVIDUTT SHARMA

Thoughts are infinite but remember actions are finite. Be ready to win with this equation.

You need to be distinct and create your own identity even if you look similar to others in the group.

When you are hurt by someone it's better to cry and mourn once rather than hold the balloon of grief and carry the baggage of pain throughout your life.

Opportunity says, 'Do not let me Go' every time it meets you. Be quick to grab it.

You need to start somewhere if you have planned your destination. Don't expect to run faster from the first step. Build the momentum gradually.

The vibrant light of knowledge has the power to illuminate your life and the world connected.

Trust the Lord and he is always there for you holding your hand and helping you to rise.

You can figure out a way out of life complexities with a cool mind.

Make an exit from things you have been doing for years and which people have failed to appreciate time and again. Do things which can boost your self-motivation and are good for finances.

You get to know each other well when you are keenly listening to the other and speak at the right time.

Never accept defeat unless you have tried time and again.

If you like to break things, then think about breaking the existing world records in your field, which are staring and challenging you.

Money creates a divider in the relationship. With love and affection, you can come closer.

The smile is on its way back to you when you knock the door of humanity with hands of kindness and love.

You may cry when someone hurts. You may cry when you win. That's life...O dear friend.

Challenges keep coming in your path so that you don't sleep while walking on your life path.

Single seed is the mother of billions of trees. Likewise, remember the supreme soul is the father of the infinite souls. Be gratefule to the Lord for who you are.

Build trust through your deeds and expression.

It's the beauty of your mind that helps you to see everything beautiful in this world.

It's time to either do things differently or do altogether different things which can shape your future. Make the most out of your life.

The yesterday cannot be changed but if you do things right today, you can definitely change tomorrow.

Slow down a bit and see the beautiful world around you. Sometimes forget to wear your watch around your mind. It would surely change your outlook towards life.

If you want to learn in life, let the child in your psyche live forever.

The time to take that step is now and not tomorrow.

© **POSITIVE WORDS FOR YOU**
BY SANDEEP RAVIDUTT SHARMA

The fountain of peace and purity resides in your mind.

You may have millions of Dollar but not a single coin which can buy happiness.

Getting used to a particular work or a lifestyle sometimes puts you into a comfort zone. You may stop taking up new challenges, and innovation is lost forever. Attempt to come out of such situations to make your life more interesting and challenging.

As flowers always smile, likewise each one of us is blessed with some unique characteristics. Find the uniqueness and you can succeed in life.

Not every generation knows the true worth of the ideals followed by their predecessor. Only by exploring history, one can find out.

Those who shop to buy happiness most of the time returns empty-handed.

If you like building then take a vow to build a long-lasting relationship.

© POSITIVE WORDS FOR YOU
BY SANDEEP RAVIDUTT SHARMA

Don't let ego rule over you when you rise in life or don't feel drowned at your fall. Get inspiration from Nature. Rise and Fall situations are part of our life. You raise your head when you fall, to see from where you have survived. You fall on someone's feet when you rise in life to thank your motivator or mentor.

Just dive in the realm of spirituality, and you are sure to emerge as a better person than before.

The more you think in times of adversity, the lesser confidence one feels. During such times don't overthink, save your energy, try to stay positive, maintain your cool and leave it to time for taking decisions on your behalf.

Your thoughts can make or break you.

Sea appears to be Cool and calm. Those who are well aware of the mood swings of the Sea do expect it to turn violent anytime. We, humans, have inherited these qualities from the Sea.

Appreciate the knowledge of the other and suggest ways that can make their life happier and better.

The more you run after money the lesser you get hold of it. It's better you stop running and relax. Be content with whatever you have.

Soul awakens when the purity of thoughts prevails.

Golden moments are those when you feel happy and blissful.

Thanks to Mother Earth who inspires us at all times. Earth never stops its rotation around the Sun even for a second. Earth nourishes all living beings as well as carry the dead with utmost care stored in different layers.

The ocean of thoughts cannot be poured into your mind bucket in one round. You need to draw it as per your ability.

While leading the crowd, do not let your actions and behaviour change. Be who you are, and do not pretend to be someone.

Those who like to play gimmick are not the serious ones.

Schedule your steps in such a way so as to improvise your learning and understanding of the various aspects of life to achieve success.

Inspire self and others to give back more to the world and serve humanity better than before.

Get ready to grind your failures and negative thoughts once for all. Be positive always.

Be ready to shield the innocent from the cruelty of selfish and greedy ones.

You can win only when you perform better than others.

You won't need to give up in life if you wish to try again.

With positive attitude you can find happiness wherever you go.

You can cross the Ocean only when you have visualised and are eager to experience what lies beyond.

© POSITIVE WORDS FOR YOU
BY SANDEEP RAVIDUTT SHARMA

Words have the power to turn people in your favour or against.

Don't just look at the problem, thrash it with your knowledge and power of thinking.

Trust someone and get trust in return.

Dreams would remain only as dreams if you forgot to wake up in time to achieve them.

Going slow for some time is fine but not remembering to cover up the lost time is a recipe for failure. Success needs attentiveness and quick response.

Discipline ensures your win. Discipline binds all the positive forces together, and you can win in any situation.

A beautiful mind can only think positive.

You can make hundreds of plans. Lord approves only those plans which come from your heart. At times provides a better plan to execute.

Happiness makes you dance, sing, and bring you in a celebration mode.

Time is unstoppable but can be turned in your favour through focused and smart efforts.

The strong relationship is always based on trust and affection for each other.

Attract enthusiasm, energy, expertise by not only visualising but by actually learning these traits from people who are already experiencing or knows it. Energy is all around. Be ready to receive positive energy to achieve things in life.

Freedom means free from the dominance of any kind. Some of us occupying the power seat interpret it as Free to Dominate.

You can copy someone's voice, habit, words and behaviour but not the Soul.

Happiness rules when you are with your near and dear ones. You don't have to make effort to Smile. It automatically appears on your face.

The season of love is always there for the beautiful mind.

The richness of culture can only be felt when you personally visit a place.

To enjoy the cruise, you need to leave the shore.

© **POSITIVE WORDS FOR YOU**
BY SANDEEP RAVIDUTT SHARMA

At times when you feel that the world is not enough for you and you intend to do something wrong. Remember that the world is within you, and it has the solution to all kinds of problems. All you need to do is focus on the present, consult your heart for what is right or wrong. Slow down your mind and relax. Have faith in the creator and let the time pass as you watch.

Without trust, nothing in this world can work.

You may rise in life just like a plane in the Sky. In both the cases you can't keep flying as it is not natural, you have to touch base once in a while either as per your own will or else gravity pulls you down.

The glow of the sun is visible even when Sun itself is playing hide and seek. Likewise, your positivity can light up the entire environment around you.

Get rid of the greed to maximise what you have unless its knowledge.

If you believe in the creator then it's quite imperative to know that everyone on this earth is here for a purpose. If God has made you rich it doesn't mean you have to go all out and distribute your wealth to the poor and become poor in a day. In my view, it means God has designated you as custodian of wealth. Your implied task or duty would be to use this wealth not only for your own consumption but provide to those who need your timely help.

Share happiness, joy and warmth and it comes back to you multiplying each time.

Hard times in anyone's life are not a permanent fixture. Face it with a smile, and it will go.

World smiles at you every day. It's only you who keep making faces, sometimes happier and at other times sad.

Distant light signifies hope. Darkness close by is the reality. Embrace reality with a glimmer of hope and you could win.

Be brave and take the risk if opportunity keeps passing your way.

Roses are waiting for those who would like to sit and resolve issues amicably.

The path may not always be smooth for you. Be confident and never lose your patience.

Happiness comes from living a life whose rules are set by you. But this cannot happen always as we live in a connected world. Find a way which satisfies all.

Shake the world to get what you have worked for.

Emotions matter the most even when you have scaled the highest peak of your life.

Awaiting baggage of uncertainty or box full of surprises. Life gives you what you have asked for.

Be grateful to the lord for what you have rather than crying over what you do not have. Gratitude brings abundance to your door step.

Views and thoughts can never be one-sided.

No one can stop your winning streak if you have delivered with disciplined and unique efforts.

You meet people not always by choice.

Say Goodbye to problems and start afresh with solutions.

Bright Sun sends its rays to illuminate the world without any kind of expectation from the recipient. Do not have any return expectations when you give a helping hand.

The golden period comes in everyone's life. It all depends on how you make the most out of it without wearing ego and selfishness.

Sharing and caring don't require too much money but a bigger and kinder heart.

www.ingramcontent.com/pod-product-compliance
Lightning Source LLC
Chambersburg PA
CBHW070803220526
45466CB00002B/529